Copyright © 2021 Garmin International, Inc.
1200 E. 151st Street, Olathe, KS, 66062
Garmin.com

ISBN: 978-0-578-85911-8
Printed in Canada

Library of Congress Control Number: 2021905871

Women of Adventure

BEING BRAVE
IN A BIG WORLD

There's a spirit of adventure in all of us.
It's what keeps us exploring and braving
truths about ourselves and the world around us.
We hope this collection of true stories about
some women we know inspires the next
generation of bold females.

Based on the Garmin Women of Adventure series.
Garmin.com/WomenOfAdventure

Written by Rebecca Sommers,
copywriter for Garmin and mother of three.

Illustrated by Adam Bowlin,
art director for Garmin and father of two.

REBECCA RUSCH

ENDURANCE ATHLETE

Rebecca Rusch grew up near a big city. She loved to play outside and ride her bike up and down the busy sidewalks. When Rebecca got a little older and went to a new school, she joined the cross country running team. She felt proud to wear her uniform as she raced through the hilly courses.

After college Rebecca kept trying new sports, like rock climbing, white water rafting and mountain biking. Then she started doing adventure races with a team — even races that were shown on T.V. An adventure race is an event that combines multiple sports and sometimes crazy stunts, like riding a camel. Rebecca and her teammates had to use maps and other tools to find their way and race through faraway places like the jungles of Borneo and the mountains of Patagonia.

Rebecca kept racing and winning. The longer and harder the race, the better she did. Her favorite events were mountain bike races that went all through the day and night.

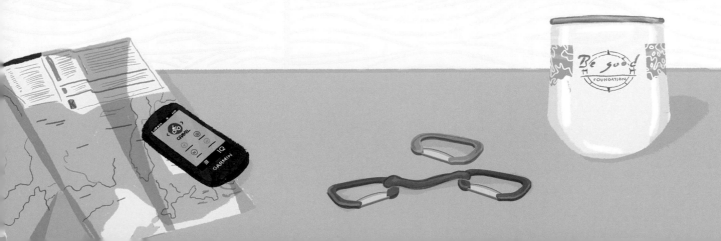

LAOS

TÂN KỲ

VIETNAM

CAMBODIA

HO CHI MINH CITY

One day Rebecca decided it was time to use all her skills to plan her biggest adventure yet — riding her bike 1,200 miles through tangled jungle trails in Vietnam and Laos. She invited another bike rider from Vietnam to join her, and the two women rode as a team and kept each other company for the long and difficult journey.

Today Rebecca teaches others about riding mountain bikes, preparing for bike packing trips and protecting the trails. Her motto is "be good." Rebecca encourages everyone she meets to take care of our world so we can explore it on two wheels or our own two feet.

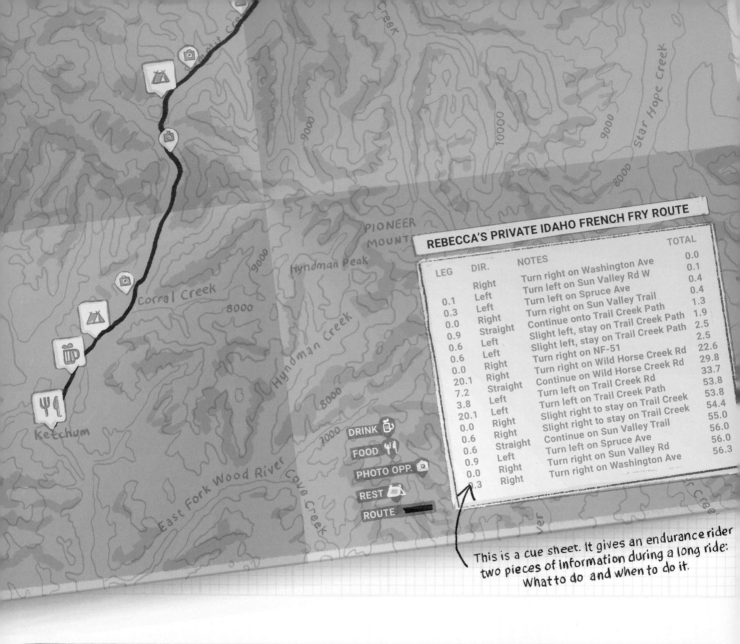

10000

9000

Star Hope Creek

8000

9000

PIONEER
MOUNT...

Hyndman Peak

Corral Creek

8000

Hyndman Creek

8000

7000

Ketchum

East Fork Wood River

Cove Creek

REBECCA'S PRIVATE IDAHO FRENCH FRY ROUTE

			TOTAL
LEG	DIR.	NOTES	0.0
	Right	Turn right on Washington Ave	0.1
0.1	Left	Turn left on Sun Valley Rd W	0.4
0.3	Left	Turn left on Spruce Ave	0.4
0.0	Right	Turn right on Sun Valley Trail	1.3
0.9	Straight	Continue onto Trail Creek Path	1.9
0.6	Left	Slight left, stay on Trail Creek Path	2.5
0.6	Left	Slight left, stay on Trail Creek Path	2.5
0.0	Right	Turn right on NF-51	22.6
20.1	Right	Turn right on Wild Horse Creek Rd	29.8
7.2	Straight	Continue on Wild Horse Creek Rd	33.7
3.8	Left	Turn left on Trail Creek Rd	53.8
20.1	Left	Turn left on Trail Creek Path	53.8
0.0	Right	Slight right to stay on Trail Creek	54.4
0.6	Right	Slight right to stay on Trail Creek	55.0
0.6	Straight	Continue on Sun Valley Trail	56.0
0.9	Left	Turn left on Spruce Ave	56.0
0.0	Right	Turn right on Sun Valley Rd	56.3
0.3	Right	Turn right on Washington Ave	

DRINK

FOOD

PHOTO OPP.

REST

ROUTE

This is a cue sheet. It gives an endurance rider
two pieces of information during a long ride:
what to do and when to do it.

LET'S EXPLORE MAPS AND WAYFINDING

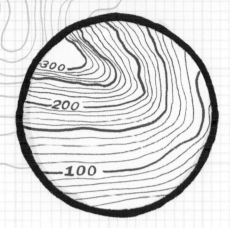

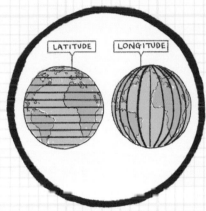

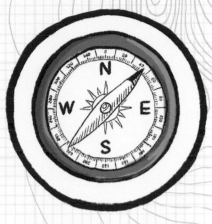

Rebecca uses topographic maps with squiggly lines that show the location and shape of mountains and lakes.

Latitude and longitude are imaginary lines used to mark the exact location of any point on earth.

A compass shows what direction you're heading at all times. It has a magnetic needle that always points north.

HOW DO YOU GET THERE?

In ancient times, people looked to the stars to help them find their way. There have been many inventions since then to guide ships, planes, vehicles, hikers and bikers. The most accurate invention is the global positioning system (GPS). It's a network of satellites that sends out a signal. GPS receivers in watches, phones and other devices decode the signals to figure out your position anywhere in the world. Can you think of some other ways GPS can help people?

PATRICIA WALSH

WALSH

ATHLETE WITH BLINDNESS

When Patricia Walsh was a little girl, she took a ferry boat ride across the Puget Sound. Her dad and sister squealed in excitement at a seal swimming alongside the boat. Patricia saw no seal. They must be playing a trick on me, she thought. But the seal was real. Patricia's dad soon realized there was a problem with her vision.

By age 14, Patricia had gone completely blind. But she kept challenging herself and dreaming big dreams. Patricia knew she needed to study hard so she could go to college and have a career someday.

Patricia studied electrical engineering and computer science in college. She even worked with a professor to make computer programs easier for people with blindness to use. One day she went for her first run on a nearby trail. Because Patricia couldn't see, she used her feet and the grassy edge of the trail to guide her path and find her way back home.

Patricia started running more and more because it made her feel good and proved she could learn new things. Sometimes she stumbled and fell, but she always got back up. The longer Patricia ran, the more her confidence bloomed. One day a friend dared her to race a triathlon. So she signed up for the longest triathlon of all — 2.4 miles of swimming, 112 miles of biking and 26.2 miles of running!

She kept racing and setting records. She even competed for the United States at the Paralympics. The Paralympics is a sporting event for athletes with disabilities.

Today Patricia lives in big cities like New York and London. She learns the city and how to get places by the subway or bus using maps and voice directions on her phone and computer. Patricia's new favorite sport is rowing, and she trains and competes with a women's team. She wants to show others that everything is possible.

SIGHT

TASTE

SMELL

SOUND

TOUCH

LET'S EXPLORE THE SENSES

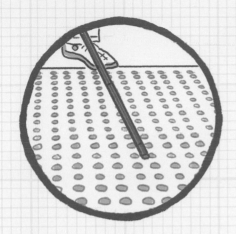

Patricia knows where the sidewalk ends and the street begins when her cane **touches** small bumps in the pavement at street crossings.

Sounds like the ding of an elevator and the honk of a horn help people with blindness **hear** what's around them and how far away the objects are.

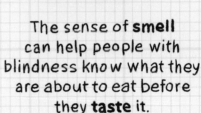

The sense of **smell** can help people with blindness know what they are about to eat before they **taste** it.

HOW CAN TECHNOLOGY HELP?

Your five senses help you notice the world around you. People with blindness don't have their sense of sight. Assistive technology in phones and computers helps them function just like people who have their sight. Some computers have a voiceover feature that translates written words and pictures into spoken words. They also have a dictation feature that turns speech into written words. Mapping apps on a phone with GPS can speak directions. The directions change as the destination gets closer. Patricia can go anywhere in the world and be fully independent with these tools. Can you walk from your bedroom to the kitchen using all your senses except sight?

MIRNA VALERIO

TRAIL RUNNER

Mirna Valerio grew up in Brooklyn, New York. One summer her parents let her go to a sleep-away camp. Mirna couldn't wait for camp to start. And after she got there, she never wanted it to end. Canoeing and swimming in the lake, hiking on mossy forest paths and singing around the campfire were Mirna's favorite activities.

In high school, Mirna went to a boarding school like most of her friends. On the first day, the students got to pick a team sport. Mirna and her friend decided to try field hockey. The coach told all the girls to run two miles. It was hard at first, but Mirna's teammates and coach cheered her on, so she kept going.

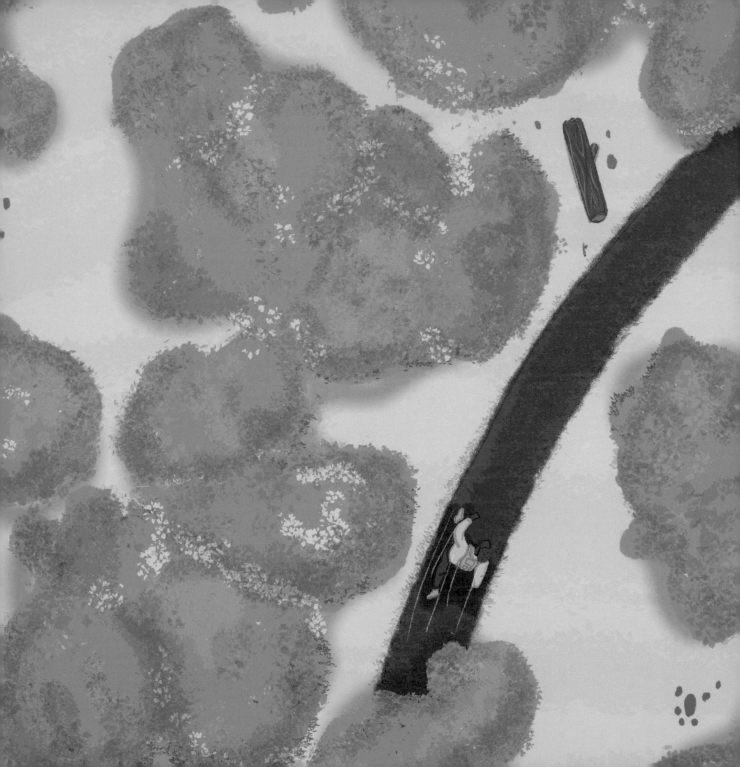

One day a friend invited Mirna to run her first ultra trail race. An ultra is a race that is longer than 26.2 miles. Sometimes the race is as far as 50 miles, 100 miles or even 200 miles. It can be lonely and dark, and she has to eat and drink along the way. Mirna's first race was hard, but the other runners and volunteers said encouraging things to her. She finished the race last, but that didn't matter. Even though her feet and her legs and her arms and her back were very tired, Mirna's heart was very happy.

Mirna runs ultra races all over the world — on the tops of volcanoes, over mountains and across islands. Sometimes she brings along other girls who love to travel and run for fun. Mirna teaches them that no matter if you are fast or slow, dark-skinned or fair, tiny or not, any body can run.

A backpack for running or hiking can hold all the important things needed for a long day on the trail. Some even store water and have a very long straw so explorers can sip without stopping.

LET'S EXPLORE TRAIL PREPARATIONS